Manage teams successfully
successfully

Manage teams successfully

How to work with others and come up with results

A & C Black • London

© A & C Black Publishers Ltd 2007

First published in 2007 by
A & C Black Publishers Ltd
38 Soho Square
London W1D 3HB

A CIP record for this book is available from the British Library.

ISBN-10: 0–7136–8154–3
ISBN-13: 978–0–7136–8154–3

Design by Fiona Pike, Pike Design, Winchester
Typeset by RefineCatch Limited, Bungay, Suffolk
Printed in Italy by Rotolito

This book is produced using paper that is made from wood grown in managed, sustainable forests. It is natural, renewable and recyclable. The logging and manufacturing processes conform to the environmental regulations of the country of origin.

Contents

What sort of team leader are you?

Answer the questions and work out your score, then read the guidance points.

Are you a good team leader?
a) No   b) Potentially   c) Absolutely

What should a good leader be?
a) Friendly   b) Reliable   c) In control

Which of these best describes your team?
a) Intimidating   b) Friendly   c) Troublesome

If your team is experiencing problems, what do you do?
a) Leave them to it
b) Talk to them, so we can work it out together
c) Step in and take charge of the problem

How well does your team work together?
a) Okay . . .
b) We get on really well together
c) Fine, if they do what's asked of them

Be honest: how do you think you could improve as a leader?

a) Be more confident
b) Get to know the team better
c) Put less pressure on myself

How do you motivate your team to work?

a) I'm not sure!
b) Keep the channels of communication open
c) Give them constant feedback

How does conflict make you feel?

a) Upset   b) Guilty   c) Driven

What's your view of communication?

a) I wish I was better at it
b) It's what holds my team together
c) I'm prepared to sacrifice it if the job gets done

How do you communicate with your team?

a) I'm there for them if they need me
b) We give each other regular updates
c) Meetings, memos, progress reports—you name it, I use it!

Do you delegate?

a) Not as much as I should
b) Yes
c) Not often—it's usually easier to do it myself

What is the usual cause of conflict in your team?

a) When tensions escalate

b) Personality clashes

c) When members don't pull their weight

a = 1, b = 2, c = 3. Now add up your scores.

- **12–19**: You seem to suffer from a lack of confidence. Being a leader is tricky for anyone at first, but with practice you can improve and succeed. Read chapter **1** for some confidence-building basics. You must get to know your team better: read chapter **2** for a formal approach, and chapter **5** for tips on motivating your team. Remember that communication is essential—chapter **6** suggests the best approaches.

- **20–29**: You're great at communicating, but watch that you're not too informal. As well as motivating your team (chapter **5**), you need to be able to step back and lead. Ensure that everyone is clear about their role by following the steps in chapter **3**, and don't be afraid of conflict—chapter **8** will show you how to make the best of it.

- **30–36**: Your problem is not a lack of confidence: in fact, you have so much that you risk intimidating and even alienating your team. Remind yourself of the qualities of a great team leader by reading chapters **1** and **4**, and read chapter **6** for advice on communicating in a more positive way. You will take pressure off yourself by delegating effectively; read about the benefits and techniques in chapter **7**.

Understanding what makes a good leader

Most people work as part of a team at some point. Teams are a great way of bringing together the skills and expertise of a group of people so that a project can be tackled in the most efficient way. Having said that, with different personalities and (often) agendas to manage, things can get tense. If you've recently taken charge of a team, this book will help you clarify your goals, pick the right people, and smooth over tensions so that your team stands the best chance of achieving its aims.

Part of being a great team leader is, of course, knowing how to lead. There are rafts of heavyweight management tomes about this very topic, but a lot of it boils down to common sense. If you're reading this book you're probably either managing a team for the first time (in which case, congratulations!), or want to refresh your skills.

It's true that some people are naturally better suited to leadership roles than others; but the good news is that the necessary skills *can* be learned. In this chapter we'll discuss practical ways to help boost your confidence in your role as the head of a team.

Step one: Understand that there are different types of leader

As you'd imagine, there are as many different types of leadership styles as there are people's personalities. For example, think of three shepherds.

- The first opens the gate and walks through, allowing the flock to follow. This shepherd **leads from the front**.
- Another stands behind the sheep and pushes or guides them through, demonstrating a **supportive leadership style**.
- The third moves from front to back and sometimes to the middle of the flock, demonstrating an **interactive leadership style**.

TOP TIP

Being flexible is key to good management. For leaders to exist, there must be followers, and the needs of followers change depending on the context. Knowing how to apply different leadership styles can help you respond equally effectively in many different kinds of situations.

Another school of thought recognises four leadership styles:

- directive
- process-driven
- creative
- facilitative

Each one is related to a personality trait. Being more relaxed doesn't necessarily mean you can't be a leader—in fact, it's a positive boon in some circumstances—it just means that you have a natural tendency towards a certain type of leadership. As you become more confident and practised in leadership, you may be able to learn other styles—more dominant, intuitive, or structured, for example. Try to work with your preferred style until you're comfortable enough to branch out.

Clearly, certain styles are suited to particular situations. For example, a structured leader is likely to succeed in a situation where process is important, such as running a complex project. The relaxed or facilitative leader may be one who manages a professional group of people, while dominant leaders may be needed in businesses where there is a real drive or need for change.

Transferring your skills between different arenas

Don't worry if you feel more comfortable in some situations than you do in others. As you gain more experience and practice, you'll see that your skills begin to transfer across the different strands of your working life.

For example, let's say you can command an audience easily when you make presentations, but don't know if you'll be able to do the same with the team you've just started managing.

Commanding an audience is a great skill and many leaders have it, but it's not the sole requirement. Leaders also need to be problem-solvers and have originality and flair, confidence and self-knowledge, strong interpersonal skills, the ability to listen, vision, good organisational skills, and so on. Your ability as a speaker suggests that you're articulate and self-confident. If you possess the other qualities too, you are well on the way to being the leader your employer needs.

Step two: Get some training

If the training budget in your organisation permits, a leadership course will help you gain a fuller understanding of what leadership is, and, by extension, how it will work for your business. Courses range from business theory to developing strategy to understanding business risk.

TOP TIP
Even if the benefits of some training are crystal-clear to you, it's no bad thing to spell them out clearly to your boss when you ask to

---

go on a course. A short e-mail spelling out what you and the organisation would gain from it will show that you are taking your new role seriously and that you're keen to take positive steps towards boosting your essential management skills. Appeal to your boss's pocket if you can; for example, if other colleagues might benefit from this type of training, find out if you could get a discount for a group booking.

Having well-developed commercial awareness and a good business education will not only give you confidence, but will also help you command respect from others in the organisation.

Step three: Build self-awareness

Your leadership style is the means by which you communicate. The more self-aware you are, the more effectively it will work for you. This means knowing:

- what you are like
- what your preferences are
- what your goals are
- how you are motivated to achieve them
- how other people perceive you and your goals

Numerous tests and questionnaires can be used to help you explore your personality and preferences; they are widely available online as well as from books, consultancies, and other sources. Surveys are also useful, and business schools have valuable data on expected leadership behaviours. You can combine information from all these sources to work out your own leadership profile.

Step four: Use it or lose it

Some leadership positions require you to set the objectives for others to follow. In these situations, scheduling, consultation, and the team building discussed in the following chapters are essential to success.

Leaders often need to work as intermediaries between two groups—those wanting the results (boards, investors, and so on), and those who will deliver the results. In this case you need to establish good communication channels with both parties that allow everyone to have the information they need at the right time.

The nature of the team you work with depends very much on your organisation and the type of work you do. You could, for example, work with one small 'core' team all the time, or you might need to build different teams for each different project you work on, selecting key people from across the business with the right skills to tackle the task at hand (these teams are often referred to as 'cross-functional').

If you need to put a team together from scratch, try to select a group of people that contains a good balance between competent managers and energetic, loyal team members. Teams need consistent, positive energy levels to sustain momentum, so it's critical that you choose a team based on the mix of talent required, rather than on friendships or office politics. See chapter 2 for more help on this.

If you are trying out new systems or approaches, make sure you surround yourself with the right people, create a framework for support, and document the process so you can later evaluate what you have done.

TOP TIP
Leadership opportunities often crop up unexpectedly, and if you work in a small business environment you'll come across them more frequently. As in most situations, your best bet is to start with an analysis of the situation. Decide what is needed and how you can best achieve it.

Common mistakes

✗ **You copy other leaders too closely**

People new to leadership roles may try to copy a leader they respect, because the person provides an easy model. This is understandable if you're feeling a little unsure of yourself in a new role, but you do run the risk of creating a false impression of what you are *really* like, or, worse, making yourself look foolish for trying to mimic a style that's incompatible with your own personality. Good—and genuine—leadership comes from within. Rather than slavishly follow someone else's style, understand what it is you respect in the other leader and think about how you can best display that attribute. If it doesn't work, don't be afraid to try a new approach.

✗ You don't work at it

Many people hope that they have natural leadership skills, and accept leadership positions without proper training or mental adjustment. This sink-or-swim approach works sometimes, but not always! You're much more likely to be successful if you build up leadership skills, increase your self-awareness, and evaluate what you do as you go along.

STEPS TO SUCCESS

✔ Try to be your own person. By all means observe good leaders in action and learn what you can from them, but don't mimic them. Be yourself, but get the training you need to take your skills to the next level.

✔ Remember the importance of context. There are management styles to suit many different occasions. Be flexible and be prepared to change your style depending on what you and your team need to achieve.

✔ Don't be afraid to ask for advice. Your manager, mentor, or a trusted colleague are good ports of call. Their advice, coupled with your own thoughts about how best to approach a situation will help you as you build your own 'brand' of leadership.

✔ Give yourself a chance. Your first few months in a new role, especially one with management responsibilities, can be challenging. Don't get too disheartened if things don't go to plan: reflect on them, draw out lessons to be learned, act on them as appropriate, and move on.

Useful links

Management First (Emerald):
www.managementfirst.com/experts/leadership.htm
The Leadership Trust:
www.leadership.co.uk
Mindtools.com, 'Become an exceptional leader':
www.mindtools.com/pages/main/newMN_LDR.htm
University of Exeter Centre for Leadership Development:
www.ex.ac.uk/leadership

Building a cross-functional team

Teams are made up of a range of people, each with the right skills for a particular part of the team's task. They may be drawn from different parts of your organisation, or they may come from a number of separate organisations. Teams such as this are often called 'cross-functional teams'.

It's your job to bring the group of people together and form them into an effective team which operates as one to achieve the task you have been set. Unsurprisingly, this can sometimes be tricky. However, there are a number of rules which, if followed, can make team building much easier and more likely to succeed. This chapter lays out the basics.

Step one: Identify the skills you require

Start off by identifying and engaging a team of people with the right skills and an enthusiasm for the project. Your team will probably need to come from all parts of your company, so that you get people with the right skills, and also get input and involvement from all parts of the business. You may well find that your senior stakeholder (the senior manager who has agreed to the project idea, for example) can help you find and recruit the right people.

Your team, obviously, will vary enormously depending on the size of your project and what it entails. Say, for example, you are organising an office move: you're likely to need floor planners, packers, removal men, electricians, IT people, and so on.

Step two: Get the right mix of personalities

Besides the different skills, it's also worth keeping an eye on the mix of personalities among your team members, as this can have a huge effect on whether the team functions properly or not. Have a look at the team roles described in the next chapter.

Ideally, you need a good mix of 'types' in your team (bearing in mind that people can fulfil more than one role at a time), as you're likely to have problems if you have too many of one type.

TOP TIP

Don't worry if your team does contain quite a few of the same type of people—there are ways round it. For example, you could split your team into smaller 'working parties', each of which is responsible for particular tasks that together contribute to the overall goal.

Step three: Find out about the stages of team formation

Teams go through a number of stages after they are first brought together, and these stages can be responsible for different kinds of problems or issues that arise.

Say, for example, your team is going through a sticky patch and you're having to deal with conflict and arguments. If, rather than wondering what on earth is going wrong, you recognise that this may simply be a result of the stage your team has reached, it will help you judge objectively what—if anything—needs to be done about it.

The four stages are:

- **Forming:** excitement is high; everything is new and fun; no one knows what they're doing yet.
- **Storming:** roles are assigned; personalities begin to show; uncertainty of others and their abilities can lead to

conflict, which can smoulder unless tackled promptly; people don't yet feel safe to be open and honest.

- **Norming:** confidence starts to improve; relationships strengthen; differences of opinion are respected; solutions begin to develop; goals become manageable, and everyone starts to work together to achieve them.
- **Performing:** the team becomes fluid, with people taking it in turns to lead; delegation occurs, so team members grow and flourish; goals and targets are reached regularly and effectively.

Step four: Help the 'norming' process along

In any team, it is important to get the 'vectors' aligned. A vector is a force that pulls in a certain direction and every project team member will have their own, created by their individual beliefs, thoughts, and desires. Within a team, it can be disastrous if everyone's vectors are all straining in different directions—and even one 'anti-vector' or team member forcing the current a separate way will have an adverse effect.

In your role as team leader, it's your responsibility to get everyone pulling in the same direction to achieve the project goals—a process known as 'vectorship'. Although this sounds obvious, it's extraordinary how many projects fail because individuals who are being negative are allowed to go unchallenged!

The best way to get these vectors aligned is to create a working climate in which mistakes and failures are viewed as learning experiences, not occasions for blame, and where every member feels included in 'the loop'. There are a number of elements which contribute to an atmosphere of this type:

✔ **a free flow of information.** Make sure that every member receives/has easy access to any information they need to do their job.

✔ **open communication.** Don't keep secrets, or allow team members to feel that some people are privy to information that others aren't.

✔ **frequent feedback.** People need to know how well they're doing—and if and where improvements can be made.

✔ **regular one-to-one interaction.** Talk to your team members as people, and use the time to make sure they're happy and on side.

✔ **a listening culture.** Make sure that people feel free to say what they think without fear of anger or retribution, and that they will be heard, even when they're voicing minority or unpopular views.

Step five: Learn what motivates people

Motivation is essential for people and teams to work effectively and harmoniously. Studies into what motivates people at work have revealed that motivators and demotivators are not necessarily the same thing. In other words, the things that make people feel motivated and enthusiastic are not always the same things that, if unsatisfactory, make them feel discontented and apathetic.

The table below identifies the top ten motivators for team members, and the top ten demotivators:

Motivators	Score	Demotivators	Score
Recognition	1	Relations with project manager	1
Achievement	2	Team peer relations	2
Responsibility	3	Salary	3
Team peer relations	4	Project manager's leadership	4
Salary	5	Security	5
Relations with project manager	6	Work conditions	6
Project manager's leadership	7	Organisation's policy	7
Work itself	8	Team subordinate relations	8
Advancement	9	Personal time	9
Personal growth	10	Title/status	10

Source: R.J. Yourzak, 'Motivation in the Project Environment' (1985)

These lists prove the point: some things, if they're good, are hardly noticed—but they cause high levels of dissatisfaction if they're bad. For more on motivating your team, read chapter 5.

TOP TIP

Go through your list of team members and consider what you think motivates each of them, or small groups of them if this is more appropriate. Then consider whether any of the demotivators listed are present in your project or organisation. Is there anything you can do to boost the positives and minimise the effect of the negatives?

Step six: Delegate

Delegation is another vital tool for managing your team. It's not something that everyone finds easy to start with, but it does get easier with practice and will help your project run smoothly. Chapter 7 deals with this in more detail, but here are the basic rules:

✔ Select the most appropriate person for the task. Depending on what the job is, you might not always have to delegate downwards, towards your team: you can also delegate upwards (to your manager) or sideways (to a peer).

✔ Communicate clearly to whoever will be helping you, so that he or she is clear about what they should be coming back to you with, and when.

✔ Break down tasks into manageable chunks, probably with deadlines at each stage when the other person can report back and let you know whether things are moving in the right direction.

✔ Keep proper records so you know what tasks you are delegating and to whom.

Step seven: Resolve conflict

Unresolved conflict can be very destructive, so it needs to be tackled immediately. Here's how:

1 **Recognise conflict.** Conflict can be either overt (clearly visible and stemming from an easily identifiable cause) or covert (bubbling under the surface, from a less obvious or apparently unrelated cause).

2 **Monitor the climate.** Look out for early warning signals so that you can deal with the conflict quickly, before it gets out of hand. Early action saves time and stress later.

3 **Research the situation.** Spend time finding out the true root cause of the conflict, who is involved, and what

the potential effects are. Putting yourself in other people's shoes will enable you to understand and empathise better.

4 **Plan your approach.** Encourage everyone involved to be open and understanding in the way they interact with others. It might be a good idea to ask people to write down their thoughts and feelings, so that they can express themselves logically and constructively.

5 **Tackle the issue.**

✓ Give everyone a chance to express their point of view.

✓ Avoid fight or flight: fighting back will only make the situation worse, while running away from the situation will show that you don't feel up to resolving it, and may lead to a loss of respect.

✓ Be assertive. Becoming aggressive could cause more damage, and being passive will get you nowhere.

✓ Acknowledge the views and rights of all parties.

✓ Encourage those involved to come up with their own solution—if they've created the solution, they are more likely to buy into it.

✓ Suggest a constructive way forward.

Read chapter 8 for more on defusing tense situations.

Common mistakes

✗ You don't involve your team early enough

Making too many rules and trying to impose your own plans and methods on your team without getting their input is asking for trouble. You've brought these people together for their skills—so involve them from the start. Not only will they provide information and ideas, but also they will feel as if they 'own' the plans, all of which boosts their level of commitment to them.

This doesn't mean that your projects should be planned by committee; rather that you, as manager, plan the project on the basis of all the available experience and creative ideas. Perhaps you could attempt the first level(s) of planning to help you explain the project to the team and then ask for comments. Then, using these, the final breakdown of tasks could be looked at again by the people who'll actually be carrying them out.

✗ You micromanage

Don't go there! You'll explode with the effort of trying to oversee every detail yourself, and your team will quickly lose motivation. Delegate the work and supervise it appropriately, but for heaven's sake keep your eye mainly on the overall direction of the project—the 'big picture'. As team leader, that's your job!

STEPS TO SUCCESS

✔ Identify the skills needed to make the project happen, and then find the people with those skills.

✔ Remember that a great team is made up of a *mix* of personalities. Don't just recruit people like you.

✔ Understand the different stages of team formation. You'll need to take the rough with the smooth and not panic.

✔ Create a good climate in which the team can function effectively.

✔ Recognise what factors motivate (and demotivate) people.

✔ Involve team members in decision making right from the start.

✔ Delegate!

✔ Spot conflict as early as possible, and take immediate steps to resolve it.

✔ Keep your eye on the big picture.

Useful links

Belbin Associates:
www.belbin.com
'Group dynamics: the basic nature of groups and how they develop':
www.managementhelp.org/grp_skll/theory/theory.htm
Project Smart:
www.projectsmart.co.uk
Team Technology:
www.teamtechnology.co.uk

Clarifying the roles within a team

So now you've built your team. Whatever the task in hand, in order for you to have the best chance of succeeding, two factors need to be in place:

- ✔ the purpose, objective or goal of the team needs to be explained clearly and adopted by all team members
- ✔ the function and tasks of each team member need to be agreed and made known

However, meeting these criteria doesn't guarantee success. As team leader, it's crucial that you forge a good combination of different behavioural types and make sure that they work together effectively.

It's up to you to focus on the behaviours of individual team members and the roles they are likely to fulfil in order to ensure that the team 'chemistry' is in place. Read on for some advice on this tricky topic.

Step one: Be aware of team role models

Increasingly, modern organisations use 'transient teams', which form and disperse on a project-by-project basis. As a result, organisations are turning towards team role models in an attempt to ensure the effectiveness of these temporary teams.

TOP TIP

A team role describes the way we behave, contribute, and relate to others in a team. It is likely to be a reflection of our natural characteristics in other workplace settings, so it is unlikely to be a surprise to you or your team colleagues. Knowing your own preferred team role and sharing this with other team members helps to manage expectations, builds trust, and aids good communication.

Step two: Identify your own role and those of your colleagues

Meredith Belbin, the business writer and academic, identified several common team roles as part of his research in the 1970s. Have a look at the table below and see if one of the roles describes your preferred behaviours. Then think about your colleagues and work out their preferred roles.

Team role	Contribution	Allowable weakness
1. Innovator	Creative, imaginative, unorthodox. Solves complex problems.	Ignores incidentals. Too preoccupied to communicate effectively.
2. Ambassador	Extrovert, enthusiastic, communicative. Explores opportunities and understands external environment. Develops contacts.	Over-optimistic. Loses interest once initial enthusiasm has passed.
3. Co-ordinator/ Leader	Mature, confident, a good chairperson. Clarifies goals, promotes decision-making, delegates well.	Can be seen as manipulative. Hurts personal work.
4. Challenger	Challenging, dynamic, thrives on pressure. Rocks the boat. Has the drive and courage to overcome obstacles.	Prone to provocation. Hurts people's feelings.

5. Judge/ Evaluator	Sober, strategic and discerning. Sees all options. Judges carefully.	Lacks drive and the ability to inspire others.
6. Diplomat/ Teamworker	Co-operative, perceptive, and diplomatic. Listens, negotiates, averts friction. Builds alliances in and out of the team.	Indecisive in crunch situations.
7. Implementer	Disciplined, reliable, conservative and efficient. Turns ideas into practical actions.	Somewhat inflexible. Slow to respond to new possibilities.
8. Outputter	Painstaking, conscientious, anxious. Searches out errors and omissions. Focuses on tasks and results, and delivers on time.	Inclined to worry unduly. Reluctant to delegate. Can be intolerant of other people.
9. Specialist	Single-minded, dedicated. Provides knowledge and skills in short supply and a professional viewpoint, often from an external source (e.g. IT, accountancy).	Contributes on only a narrow front. Dwells on technicalities.

Team role	Contribution	Allowable weakness
10. Supporter/ mediator	Focuses on team relationships. Builds morale, resolves conflict, gives advice, supports and encourages.	Can be seen as interfering.
11. Quality controller	Ensures tasks are done well. Checks output and focuses on quality.	Preoccupied with high standards; can lack vision.
12. Reviewer	Monitors performance. Observes and reviews performance, promotes feedback, looks for pitfalls.	Preoccupied with end result; unaware of the nitty-gritty.

These designations fall into three categories: the action-oriented roles, the people-oriented roles and the cerebral roles. The action-oriented roles are numbers 4, 7, 8, and 12. The people-oriented roles are numbers 2, 3, 6, and 10. The cerebral roles are numbers 1, 5, 9, and 11.

By understanding your preferred team role, as well as those of your colleagues, you are able to adapt to the demands placed upon you. As these roles describe behaviour and not knowledge or skills, it's likely that your preferred team role will fluctuate over time along with changes in circumstances.

The context in which the team exists, the external pressures that are placed upon it, and your own personal motivations are all likely to affect your preference.

You may find that, over time, your team role preference develops. This may happen quite naturally, as a result of experience, or as a result of the particular demands of a situation. You may also choose to focus on a role that you would like to try out, and make conscious changes (although it often helps if you have a strong motive to do so). Whether you are taking on a role that comes naturally to you or are trying out a new one, let your colleagues know your plans so that they know how to relate to and engage with you.

TOP TIP

Although you may have lots of experience in one particular role, as you progress in your career it's a good idea to take a different role from time to time so that you can learn new skills and begin to understand the different role dynamics from first-hand experience.

The table above shows information on individuals' strengths, interpersonal skills, and team-building skills as well as their organising and decision-making abilities. This cocktail of information will help you to put together a well-balanced team.

Step three: Avoid unbalanced teams

Teams will perform inefficiently when there is an unequal distribution of team roles. For example, if several team members have the same preference for a particular role, they'll end up competing for it. This may result in tension, conflict, and poor decision making. If you find yourself in a situation like this, try to get to grips with team dynamics and call a brief meeting to clear the air. Make the team realise that you're aware of the tensions, but that everyone has to get over themselves and adapt so that all roles are covered.

TOP TIP
Be open about the way you identify the roles and how you assign them to team members. Roles don't have to be imposed by the team leader; it can be done co-operatively.

Step four: Understand the alchemy of high-performing teams

At the beginning of this chapter we mentioned the term 'chemistry'. It's important to remember that the forces that hold teams together go beyond individual preferences for particular roles. It's necessary to create connections between team members that lead to commitment, respect and responsibility.

Factors that contribute to high-performing teams are:

✔ good communication

✔ the courage to confront conflict

✔ the ability to give feedback

✔ the ability to empathise with other team members

✔ a willingness among team members to put themselves at the service of the team, rather than to pursue a personal goal

---

TOP TIP

Build good team chemistry with exercises that build trust and encourage good communication and feedback. You could do this at the start—perhaps at an 'away day' which includes challenges and fun, or by meeting to formally discuss ideas and concerns. This will help the team to move through the challenges of making decisions, managing conflict, and completing tasks.

Common mistakes

✗ **You assume that everyone is content to fulfil their assigned role, for the 'greater good' of the team's overall purpose**

Consigning someone to their 'preferred role' and assuming that they are happy to continue in that role can lead to low morale and loss of dynamism. Give members of the team the chance to voice their concerns, and instil a culture of feedback so that they 'buy in' to the team's overall purpose, and no dissatisfactions fester and become destructive.

✗ You focus too much on your own role

All team members must be able to communicate well with each other, thus bridging the role boundaries. Taking responsibility for your own role AND the connection between your role and others' is key to ensuring that the team runs smoothly.

STEPS TO SUCCESS

✔ Communication, communication, communication!

✔ Be aware of your own preferences, and those of your team colleagues.

✔ Remember that, even if you are team leader, it's not all about you: you are part of the team, too!

✔ Don't impose team roles based on your preconceptions; agree roles with individuals before formalising them.

✔ By getting to know your colleagues you can judge who will work best in which role.

Useful links

Belbin Team Roles (go to the self-perception questionnaire on e-interplace®):

www.belbin.com

Working out your team role:

www.teamtechnology.co.uk/
workingoutyourteamrole.htm

Team Management Systems online:

www.tms.com.au

Developing your leadership skills

As we have seen, it can be tough getting to grips with the fact that you're now running a team, rather than just being part of one. Having built your team and clarified the roles within it, you need to start leading. This chapter will help you to build on the basics you learnt in chapter 1.

A good team leader manages to possess authority along with strong communication skills and a lightness of touch that draws the various personalities together so that they work well towards achieving their shared goals. This may initially seem a tall order, but it *is* something that can be developed through experience.

Every leader has his or her own style, and when you are developing a high-performing team this needs to combine with an understanding of:

- the benefits of good team building: what it can achieve and what the leader should be striving for
- team roles and dynamics: how teams work and achieve their greatest success
- the key stages of team development: what they are and how to support the team at each stage

- **the features of a successful team and team leader**
- **how to avoid potential problems and pitfalls**

Step one: Understand what makes a good team leader

Leadership, in broad strokes, is the capacity to establish direction and motivate others towards working for a common aim. Successful teamwork depends on the team leader's ability to make sure all team members know what that aim is and what they each need to do to achieve it.

Naturally, all teams are different and have their own dynamic, and all leaders develop their own style for forming, developing, and leading them; but good team leaders have certain characteristics in common. For a team to work, it's essential that all members are committed, so leaders must be supportive, enthusiastic, and motivational people to work with. They must organise and communicate well in order to co-ordinate team efforts both *within* the team and with others *outside* the team. During difficult or stressful times, team leaders need to be approachable; they should be good listeners who can offer feedback and advice. Turn to chapter 6 for advice on improving your communication skills.

What are the features of a good team?

It goes without saying that successful teams are ones in which people don't waste time trying to achieve success at the expense of others. Instead, they work at understanding each other, and communicate honestly and openly. They're committed to the team's success and are respectful and supportive of each other, sharing information and experiences.

Conflict is unavoidable in most work situations, but a good team will work through it and reach an understanding by generating new ideas. A good team also acknowledges the role of the leader and understands when he or she needs to act and make a decision (in an emergency, for example, or if there is a major problem or disagreement).

Step two: Focus on the work

For anyone interested in productive teamwork, it's often better to start with the work rather than the team. First of all, think about whether the job in hand really does need a team to tackle it. Some types of work, such as repetitive or unskilled tasks and, at the other extreme, specialist activities, are best performed by loners. Rounding up such people and forcing them to work as part of a team risks producing a double disadvantage: their personal productivity falls and they feel that their privacy has been invaded.

While it's currently popular to strive for an 'all-inclusive' approach in the workplace, and some people argue that isolated workers need a social dimension to their work, there are few benefits to forcing this set-up on someone. Introverts need work suitable for introverts, while extroverts need work appropriate to extroverts.

Step three: Help the team succeed

The team approach for organising work depends on empowerment—that is, making sure that each person is allowed to perform to the best of his or her abilities. This relies on trust—the confidence that a manager places on the qualities and calibre of the employees. It also depends on how well members of a group understand each other's strengths and weaknesses. That's why, if your budget allows, training in teamwork is so important and why it helps for you to understand the language of team roles.

TOP TIP
As a team leader, remember that you have
to allow team members the freedom to
do what their role entails—empower them.
Give them all the information they
need to make things happen.

Step four: Reward teams at the right time

All teams need to be assessed, but how should it be done so that it's positive and constructive? One way is to set objectives for teams and judge how well these have been met. This view is popular in the 'top-down' school of management, where, as the name would suggest, senior managers make the decisions, which are then passed down through the ranks to the employees.

The argument is that teams need fixed incentives to perform well, an assumption linked with the opposite view that without such an incentive the team won't perform well. This approach can, however, backfire. Successfully meeting given criteria depends partly on circumstances and contingencies, and may not be a completely honest reflection of effort or skill. Also, objectives may be too easy to reach, or too difficult. In the end, people may focus more on the shortcomings of the incentive than on the work they're doing. Retrospective awards for good team performance (that is, given once the project is complete) are better received than prospective rewards for teams given set targets. In larger organisations, this approach is given added impetus by performance-related bonuses.

Step five: Stick to the essentials of effective teamworking

Again, start with the work. Work out who will be doing what; also, decide which remaining tasks can be assigned to others, and make sure that those involved know that the responsibility for completing those tasks rests with them.

If possible, train your team so that it plays to the best strengths of its individual players. Make sure each person is allowed to develop ownership, pride, and maximum commitment to the team's responsibilities. One way you can do this as team leader is by delegating effectively.

Finally, understand what motivates the team—what gives it its momentum? Find out more in the next chapter.

Common mistakes

✗ You misunderstand people

While it's obviously crucial that you understand the nature of the work being undertaken, you also need to be aware of the skills, experience, and approach of those doing the work. Taking account of people's strengths, motivations, and working patterns can certainly help to build or break teams.

✗ You don't understand teams and what they need to succeed

Don't become too glib about the terminology—'team' and 'teamwork' too easily become meaningless words, so make sure you're not bandying about terms that you don't really understand. Remember to spend time evaluating the given task before you begin, and bear in mind that not everyone flourishes in a team—some people will need more support than others.

STEPS TO SUCCESS

✔ Understand what makes a good team leader.

✔ Establish direction, communicate your team's goals clearly to them, and then motivate everyone towards achieving them.

✔ Focus on the work at first, then the team.

✔ Help the team succeed by communicating effectively and understanding that you'll need to adjust your approach depending on who you're talking to.

✔ Reward teams at the right time.

✔ Stick to the essentials: think about whether the whole team need to be involved in a project at once; work out who will be doing what and when; monitor progress and offer support as necessary.

Motivating others in a team

As we have seen already, teams will often come together for a project, then, once the objectives have been met, they dissolve and their members move on to a new team with new people and a new purpose. It's therefore crucial that, as team leader, you start motivating your team from day one. Even if you are leading an established, more permanent team, motivation is key.

This chapter suggests how to give yourself the best chance of succeeding when managing a group of different personalities. If you follow these steps while building a genuine relationship with your colleagues, you'll be able to motivate them and build a high-performing team.

Step one: Remember that you're working with humans, not machines!

The thing about teams is that they are made up of people. As we have seen, the joy—and the frustration—of people is that they each have different values, beliefs, and motivations. These are not always clear-cut, but the results of thwarting someone's values and beliefs and preventing them from satisfying their motivations can range from apathy to real damage. As our values and beliefs are an intrinsic part of who we are, if we are asked to compromise them we feel that we are being asked to compromise ourselves. This often results in unexpected and, most likely, undesirable responses which destabilise the team.

TOP TIP

As a team leader, you sometimes have to support organisational objectives even when you disagree with them. Look at the bigger picture and try to consider the reasons from a wider perspective. If you still can't see the rationale, renegotiate your task or try to find something in what the team has been asked to do that motivates you. You can't expect a team to be motivated if they detect your reluctance.

Step two: Communicate your vision, mission, and purpose

In order to have a motivated, well-aligned team, you need to make sure that the team knows why it exists and what its purpose is. The vision, mission, or purpose is a statement that represents the bigger picture, making clear the ultimate reason that team members have been brought together.

Step three: Agree terms of engagement

The terms of engagement set out the 'rules' that the team will adhere to. It's best to work these out as a team, and formalise them in writing. They will then create the structure that carries the team through the difficult times when the initial excitement of its purpose has passed, relationships are strained, and tensions arise.

The terms of engagement should include:

✔ **Respect for each other:** this includes active listening, giving feedback, and valuing difference in terms of the values, skills, and talents of the different team members.

✔ **Conflict management**: although many people are conflict-averse, conflict can actually be a creative force, bringing fresh ideas and energy to a team. Remember, though, that creative conflict needs courage and openness.

✔ **Decision-making processes**: if there are divided opinions, how will this be resolved? Is the decision-making process based on one vote per person, majority rule, and a willingness to be a loyal minority? Does the team leader have a casting vote? Is consensus the only way the team will arrive at a decision?

✔ **Time management and focused commitment**: You should agree on prompt arrival at meetings, and put it into the terms of engagement. You could also formally disallow mobile phones or e-mails during meetings or team activities.

Active listening

Active listening is one of the most powerful communication tools anyone can exercise. The listener's full attention must be given to the communicator, and the listener should use active body language that demonstrates understanding, along with a non-judging acceptance of what is being said. There should be no interruptions, and only when the communicator has finished giving his or her message should the listener respond. They should respond in the first person ('I') to show that they are accepting personal responsibility for the message imparted.

Step four: Understand other people's motivations

Everyone has their own reason for contributing to a team's common purpose, and this may be different for each team member. It's important to know what the reasons are so that the allocated roles are in line with the team members' aspirations (see chapters 2 and 3 for more on this). Members may have an interest in developing new team role capabilities, in which case they may choose a role that is not in line with their preference. If so, they will need support and coaching from you as team leader.

TOP TIP

In a diverse team, members' motivations are very likely to be different so you will have to find the way that works for each person. Probably the simplest approach is to ask them!

Step five: Allocate roles and responsibilities

As explained in chapter 3, in order for a team to function effectively and efficiently, a range of different roles needs to be covered. If everyone is generating ideas, no-one will implement them. If everyone is waiting to be inspired, no inspiration will be given. If there is an imbalance in the team, you can negotiate and agree different roles, whether for the purposes of personal development or to support the overall aims of the team. By doing this openly and fairly you will keep your team members 'on side'—and therefore motivated.

Step six: Offer constructive feedback

Honest, constructive, and open communication is crucial for a high-performing team. You should clear the air regularly: nothing that should be said should be left unsaid, and feelings and ideas must be shared freely. Make time for reviews and evaluations at project milestones, and give feedback on individual contributions and performance.

Step seven: Praise achievement and celebrate success

Your role is to ensure that the team has the direction, support, and resources it needs to perform its tasks properly. You will need to step in from time to time and join with your team members as an equal. You will also need to know when to step back, create distance, and give direction, encouragement and reward. Leading a high-performing team is one of the most satisfying managerial functions you can perform and will only enhance your reputation as a leader. So, act as a role model and exhibit the behaviours you seek in your team.

It is not just the 'big' things that need to be noted and celebrated. Contributions of any size need to be encouraged through recognition and reward—which doesn't have to be financial. It's important that all the team members feel that they are valued and that they are making an important contribution. In many organisations, teams are transient and are formed and disbanded according to the organisation's needs. Building the team and winding up at the end of the project are important functions—and it's up to you as team leader to perform these.

TOP TIP
If you feel that you aren't succeeding, it's likely that you have misunderstood your colleagues' motivations. Watch them interacting and reflect on what drives and inspires them. Adjust your style to meet them.

Step eight: 'Walk the talk' and empathise with team members

Team leaders need to be able to empathise with their team members at all stages of the team formation process and to intervene when necessary to help them move through *forming*, *storming*, *norming* and *performing*. This process can be unsettling, especially as a team moves from the 'nice' phase at the beginning (*forming*) to the 'bedding down' stage (*storming*), during which personal agendas and animosities can emerge. It's important that team members can make sense of this turbulent and sometimes chaotic time and move into the more creative phases (*norming* and *performing*). Keeping firm hold of the reins during the tricky times requires courage but will reap rewards in the end.

Common mistakes

✗ You try to be 'one of the crowd'

This is a common mistake among team leaders, when in fact they should step back and provide the context and resources to enable the team to function effectively. It's sometimes difficult, especially if you have been promoted from within the team, to establish enough distance to gain respect and to maintain sufficient closeness to preserve relationships. It is a balancing act—but however you decide to do it, remain open and honest so that your team know what you are doing and can help you in achieving your aims.

✗ You're afraid of conflict

Trying to impose rules that prevent conflict from happening can stem the creative potential of a team. Conflict often engenders a feeling of being out of control, and this can be scary for team leaders. However, by creating and agreeing a process to manage and resolve conflict you can help the team to reach new heights of creativity. This can be done when you are forming the terms of engagement.

✗ You shy away from challenges

Teams can become disheartened—and less productive—when they are working in a challenge-free environment. Sometimes, team leaders have to inject a challenge or create a crisis in order for the energy to return and for the team to refocus. There is nothing like a common 'enemy' to raise the temperature again!

STEPS TO SUCCESS

✓ Don't forget that you're working with a group of *individuals*.

✓ Keep a professional distance—but don't be cold and distant.

✓ Create—and use—terms of engagement.

✓ At the start, agree how decisions will be made.

✓ Have a clear conflict management strategy.

✓ Keep in touch with your team members' motivations.

✔ If you need to criticise, make it *constructive criticism*.

✔ Don't forget to celebrate successes.

Useful links

'Team Motivation' by Peter Grazier:

www.teambuildinginc.com/article_teammotivation.htm

'Motivating team members through tough times':

www.lmdulye.com/Generic2-WAYCOMPASS.PDF

'How to motivate your team':

www.funevents.com/p4_motivteam.htm

'Motivation Building':

www.correllconcepts.com/Motivation-creator/
motivation-building.htm

Communicating well with your team

As we have seen, good communication is vital where teams are concerned. In fact, everything depends on it: monitoring progress, receiving early warning of problems, promoting co-operation, encouraging team involvement—you name it, good communication is central to it. How often have you heard the phrases 'due to a lack of communication', 'a breakdown in communication', or something similar? Communication is central to the way humans work: and because it comes naturally to us, we don't spend enough time thinking about how to do it properly.

The purpose of this chapter, then, is to give you some ideas and rules on how to communicate effectively within a project environment, and to flag up some of the areas in which communication can go wrong.

Step one: Take responsibility

This is probably one of the hardest messages for anyone to take on board.

The fact is that good communication is about **personal responsibility**: your message can only be understood properly if you, the communicator, take full responsibility for how it is styled and structured. In other words, if somebody misunderstands your message or reacts badly to it, it is not usually their fault. They're not difficult or obstinate . . . it's just that *you* didn't find the right way of presenting the message to them!

The good thing about this is that, if you don't get it right the first time, all you have to do is go on doing different things until you do get the response you want.

Once you have fully grasped how true this is, the results—in terms of improvements in team morale and mutual understanding—can be amazing.

Step two: Recognise that different people understand in different ways

One essential part of working well with your team is communicating clearly with them. It is also useful to know that different people absorb information in different ways. So when you're communicating, it's important to do so in a manner that gets through to as many people as possible.

Research into learning styles during the 1970s established that people fall into four main categories:

1 **'Why?' people:** who want all the reasons for doing something

2 **'What?' people:** who want all the facts about it

3 **'How?' people:** who want only the information they need to get on and do it

4 **'What if?' people:** who are more interested in the consequences of doing it

It was also found that if any of these kinds of people don't get the type of information they naturally prefer, they tend to switch off. So, every presentation, information booklet, team talk, or other method of communication you use has a much better chance of being heard and absorbed by everyone in your team if it contains all four elements.

TOP TIP

It's also worth remembering a very useful concept known as the 'three times convincer'. This is based on the fact that 80 per cent of people need to hear a message three times before they buy into it; 15 per cent need to hear it five times; and five per cent up to 25 times! With this in mind, then, messages should be restated at least three times, preferably in different ways, with a few days between each time.

Step three: Study your forms

There are three primary forms of communication: verbal, non-verbal, and written.

✔ **Verbal.** The majority of our communication is done this way, and there are lots of advantages: it's fast, easy, and natural, for example. The disadvantage is that the words 'disappear' once spoken, and conversations often get remembered in different ways by different participants—if at all! If you're not careful how you use it, the spoken word is most likely to get you into trouble.

✔ **Non-verbal.** Body language and other types of non-verbal communication are valuable ways of boosting a message. If you're committed to something, the passion and enthusiasm you show with your gestures and demeanour make what you say all the more compelling. Non-verbal communication usually accompanies the verbal, and is a valuable way of adding to a message. However, if it contradicts your words it can give away your true feelings; it's therefore important to learn to control it, in order to use its full power.

✔ **Written.** Written communication is much more permanent and, for many people, carries a lot more weight. It has the advantage of being independent of individual memories, but if it's badly phrased, it can still be ambiguous and open to misinterpretation.

TOP TIP

Informal communication is normally verbal, and (except for telephone communication) includes body language. Formal communication contains a greater proportion of written material, often because people need to keep records. In formal communication, it's best to back up a verbal exchange with subsequent written confirmation of what was said.

Step four: Choose your channels

You can combine the three basic forms into an infinite variety of shades and applications, and these can be further extended by the choice of channels used to pass the message on to others. Here are just some of the channels available to most team leaders:

- newsletters
- memos
- contracts
- team meetings
- presentations
- progress reports
- phone conversations
- faxes

- e-mail
- letters
- drawings
- one-to-one meetings
- specifications
- training courses
- video conferencing
- the internet

Each of these contains one or more of the three primary forms in different combinations. Some are more appropriate to formal communications, and others to informal ones, but most can be adapted to suit specific circumstances.

Step five: Differentiate between active and passive communication

One common problem in today's workplace is information overload—there's so much stuff flying around that people need to know or read, that they don't know where to start. A good way of alleviating this is to draw a distinction between 'active' and 'passive' channels of communication. Active channels are those which demand someone's attention (such as the telephone); passive channels are those that are there for when they're needed (a newsletter, for example).

You can use the former for communication that requires action, and the latter for material that's 'for information only'. However, you can use an active channel to draw attention to a passive channel—for example, an e-mail telling everyone to look at the latest newsletter.

Step six: Manage your meetings

Meetings are one of the most common—and useful—forms of communication in any team. This is because they can cover almost any situation you're likely to encounter, and will fit both formal and informal occasions. For example:

- **One-to-ones.** Normally held weekly with individual team members, these informal meetings are ideal for motivating people, catching up on progress, and making sure that any problems are identified and dealt with as early as possible.
- **Full team meetings.** These are held regularly (fortnightly or monthly, perhaps) so that all team members can update each other on what's happening within each area, identify gaps or slippage in schedules, and be sure that all parts of the 'big picture' come together.
- **Presentations.** These are more formal affairs, often held to impart messages to key stakeholders—such as the users, project sponsor, or shareholders—to keep them informed and on side.

There is a big 'but', though. Meetings are useful, but only if they're run properly and are held only when necessary. If not, they can be a complete waste of time and resources. Below is a list of golden rules. Not all will apply to all meetings, but they're useful general guidelines:

✔ Make sure that the meeting has properly set objectives.

✔ Make certain that everyone knows what they are required to contribute, then develop an agenda and circulate it in advance so that all attendees can prepare.

✔ Start on time—waiting for latecomers only rewards their bad time-keeping.

✔ Deal with one agenda item at a time, though be flexible about order if changes would be helpful.

✔ Encourage all members to contribute—don't take silence as agreement, and don't allow one person to dominate.

✔ Don't allow 'multiple meetings' (that is, people holding discussions between themselves) or interruption of the speaker.

✔ After discussion, test for the readiness to make a decision, make it, then check commitment to the decision.

✔ Assign actions and agree deadlines.

✔ Summarise the decisions and actions at the end of the meeting.

✔ Agree the time and place of the next meeting, and finish as close to the planned time as possible.

TOP TIP
Some managers make use of '60-second meetings'. This might sound bizarre, but it really can work. Try getting your team

---

**together for 60 seconds at the beginning of
the day, and maybe at lunchtime and close
of business as well. A lot can be said in
60 seconds—to set the day up, for example—
and it can add buzz and improve teamwork.**

Step seven: Identify the barriers to communication

Another useful aspect to remember is that communications generally have a number of barriers to pass through, in the course of which messages can get filtered, re-interpreted, or diluted. Recognising these barriers is important, as it's then possible for you to decide when communications need to be followed up, reiterated, or reinforced in some way.

Barriers divide roughly into four main categories: environmental, background, personal, and organisational.

■ **Environmental.** These include factors such as noise, temperature, air quality, location, and the immediate surroundings (cramped, spacious, tidy/messy, and so on). Each of these has an effect not only on people's ability to communicate but also on their enthusiasm and motivation. Try to be sensitive to their reactions, and if environmental factors are having an adverse effect, do something to remedy the problem.

- **Background.** We all encode our thoughts and interpret other people's meanings on the basis of our own cultural, social, and educational backgrounds. Among a diverse group of people, this can cause all sorts of problems. Imagine inviting a group of colleagues to meet you for dinner, for example; they all turn up in the evening, but you meant lunch! A very common instance is jargon—every organisation has its own, and it's easy to forget that outsiders might not understand, or think that something different is meant. Team members from different cultural backgrounds are likely to have similar problems. It's a difficult hurdle to get round, but do try to make sure that everyone is clear at all times about what is intended by a particular message.

- **Personal.** Tiredness, hunger, thirst, and other temporary conditions are barriers to communication, as are personal prejudices and circumstances. Again, these can be difficult to overcome, but try to be aware of them: for instance, if someone arrives late for an appointment and is looking harassed, it's not a good time to ask 'Can I just have five minutes before you go?' Don't expect your message to be well received, or even heard!

- **Organisational.** Rank and status are the obvious examples of this kind of communications barrier: a person who is your senior stakeholder will react differently to you than your recently recruited office junior, for example. Again, being aware of this will help you to frame your communication appropriately, to give it the best chance of getting through.

Common mistakes

✗ You don't have a communications plan

You might have a brilliant grasp of how to use different forms and channels of communication, and an excellent understanding of your team members as people. But if you don't have a proper communications plan, you're likely to find there are all sorts of gaps in who knows what, regardless of how effective each individual piece of communication is. Right from the outset, therefore, you need to plan who needs to know what, when, and in how much detail. Then stick to the plan and make sure you don't miss bits out.

✗ You choose the wrong form

A casual chat with your boss about an interesting idea is *not* a proper basis on which to kick off a project. You need a formal project specification that has been thrashed out and agreed upon by all parties. And asking someone in an apparently friendly way if you can 'just have five minutes', while looming over their desk with your arms folded and your brow furrowed, will make them feel that this is an order, not an invitation. Be careful that you use the different forms appropriately, according to whether a situation needs to be formal or informal, setting out boundaries, or merely creating atmosphere.

STEPS TO SUCCESS

✔ Take responsibility for communication—if people don't react in the way you want, don't blame them, just do it differently.

✔ Remember that different people understand things in different ways, and adjust how you present information accordingly.

✔ Understand the three primary forms of communication, and remember that they suit formal and informal situations in different ways.

✔ Choose which channels you're going to use to get your messages across to people.

✔ Reduce information overload by using active and passive communication channels, or a combination of both, as you need to.

✔ Manage meetings properly to reduce time wasting and increase effectiveness.

✔ Identify and work round barriers to communication.

✔ Have a proper communications plan, so that nothing gets omitted.

Delegating without guilt

For you and your team to work together most effectively, you need to get to grips with delegation. It's a key skill to develop. Delegation isn't about giving tasks to others because you can't be bothered to do them yourself—it's about getting a particular job done, but it's also about encouraging people to learn new skills and reach their potential, all of which helps a business to grow.

For many of us, it seems to be a natural tendency to want to be in control of everything. We find it difficult to let go of things we know we can do well ourselves. If you want to be a successful manager, though—and preserve your own sanity—that's exactly what you must do.

Step one: Don't fight it!

Some people do genuinely find it difficult to delegate, for a variety of reasons. Often, it seems quicker to perform the task yourself rather than to bother to explain it to somebody else and then correct his or her mistakes. You might worry that the person will make a bit of a hash of it and it'll take a long time to put right the mistakes they make. On the other hand, you may feel threatened by the competence of a person who is quick on the uptake and does well. You might worry that the employee may take over the role of being the person the rest of the staff go to with their problems. They may even find something wrong with the way *you* do things.

If you lack confidence, you may find it hard to give instructions and you'll put off delegating. If you do delegate and problems arise because the employee fails to do what you've asked him or her to do, you may doubt your own ability to confront the person about his or her actions. If staff have been given increased responsibilities and have done well, you may not be confident of being able to reward them sufficiently. You might even be reluctant to delegate tasks that you think are too dull.

Finally, you may realise that delegation is necessary, but you don't know where to start, or how to go about it. You need some kind of method to follow. The following steps will help put you on the right track.

Step two: Understand how delegation can help you

Delegation offers many benefits:

✔ It allows you to concentrate on the things you do best.

✔ It gives you the time and space to tackle more interesting and challenging tasks.

✔ You'll be less likely to put off making key decisions.

✔ You'll be much more effective overall.

Your team will benefit too; everyone needs new challenges, and by delegating to them, you'll be able to test their ability in a range of areas and increase their contribution to the business. They'll be able to take quick decisions themselves and develop a better understanding of the details involved in the process. In short, good delegation can make everyone more productive.

It's all too tempting to withdraw into 'essential' tasks and not develop relations with your team. The bottom line, though, is that it's wasteful for senior staff to be paid a lot of money for doing low-value work, and passing tasks down the line is essential if other people are to develop.

TOP TIP
Delegation doesn't make things easier—there will always be other challenges—but it does make things more efficient. Essentially, it represents a more interactive way of working with a team of people, and it involves instruction, training, and development. The results will be well worth the time and effort you invest in delegating properly.

Step three: Know when to delegate . . . and what

Delegation is such an important part of successful management that you should actively look for opportunities to do it. If you have too much work, or if you don't have enough time to devote to important tasks, delegate. When it's clear that certain staff need to develop, particularly new employees, delegate. When an employee clearly has the skills needed to perform a specific task, delegate.

Start with any routine administrative tasks that take up too much of your time. There are likely to be many small everyday jobs which you've always done. You may even enjoy doing them, but they're not a good use of your time. Review these small jobs and delegate as many of them as you can. Being your company's point of contact for a particular person or organisation may well be important, but can also be time-consuming—this is an excellent task to delegate.

On a larger scale, delegate projects that it makes sense for one person to handle; this will be a good test of how the person manages and co-ordinates the project. Give the person something he or she has every chance of completing successfully, rather than an impossible task at which others have failed and which may well prove a negative experience for the person concerned.

TOP TIP
Make an effort to delegate tasks for which a
particular team member has a special
aptitude. For example, if you have a partner
company overseas, make someone with
good language skills the new point of
contact. He or she will enjoy the chance
to use their languages more than normal,
and clients or colleagues overseas will
appreciate the fact that someone is
taking the trouble to speak to them
in their own language.

Who should I delegate to?

Make sure you understand the people you're delegating
to. They must have the skills and ability—or at least the
potential—to develop into the roles you have in mind, and
must be people you can trust. Test them out first with a
few small jobs so that you can gauge their strengths and
weaknesses. Also, make sure that the employee has time
for the assignment—the last thing you want to do is put
too much pressure on your most valuable team members.
Aim to share the delegation among as many employees
as possible, so think about the possibility of assigning a
task to two or more people.

Step four: Be positive

Think positively: you have the right to delegate and, frankly, delegate you must. You won't get it 100 per cent right the first time, but you will improve with experience. Be as decisive as you can, and if you need to improve your assertiveness skills, consider attending a course or reading one of the many books on the subject. A positive approach will also give your team members confidence in themselves, and they need to feel that you believe in them.

If you expect efficiency from the person you delegate to, you need to organise yourself first. If there's no overall plan of what's going on, it'll be hard to identify, schedule, and evaluate the work being delegated. Prepare before seeing the person (but don't use this as a ploy to delay!). Assess the task, decide how much responsibility the person will have, and keep an eye on progress.

TOP TIP
Use your common sense about how many instructions or how much detail you give about the task to be done. Depending on the type of job that needs to be done, you may not be able to be very detailed at all. If the task is a creative one, for example, you'll need to give the person you're delegating to some leeway so that they can test out a few different

approaches. If the task to be done is urgent
and critical, though, it's essential that
you're as specific as possible.

Step five: Discuss the task to be delegated

When you meet the person or people you're delegating to, discuss the tasks and the problems in plenty of detail, and explain fully what's expected of them. It's crucial to give people precise objectives, but encourage them to seek these out themselves by letting them ask you questions and participate in setting the parameters. They need to understand why they're doing the task and where it fits into the scheme of things. Ask them how they'll go about the task, and discuss their plan and the support they might need.

Step six: Set targets and offer support if necessary

Once you've discussed the details of the job to be done, agree some targets with your colleague and schedule some deadlines into your diaries. Summarise what has been agreed, and take notes about what the person is required to do, so everyone is clear. Sending a brief summary e-mail ensures that you both have a record of what's decided.

How much support you offer and give will very much depend on the person and your relationship with them. In the early stages you might want to work with him or her and to share certain tasks, but you'll be able to back off more as your understanding of the person's abilities increases. Encourage people to come back to you if they have any problems — while it's important to let them get on with things, you should be accessible if anyone has a problem or the situation changes. If someone needs to check something with you, try to get it back to him or her quickly. If things are going according to plan, don't interfere or criticise, as not only is it pointless but also you'll sap their confidence.

TOP TIP

Monitoring progress is vital. It's all too easy to forget all about the task until the completion date, but in the meantime all sorts of things could have gone wrong. When you're planning the task, build in as much time as you can to review progress. If more problems were expected to arise and nothing has been heard, check that all is well. Schedule regular update meetings with the person and be flexible enough to change deadlines and objectives as the situation changes.

Here's a quick summary of how much supervision is needed, depending on a person's experience and motivation:

Level of experience	Degree of supervision required
New or inexperienced person, low confidence	Tell the person what to do; show them how to do it; put a plan together, showing each checkpoint when they have to report back to you; and review the task and give feedback.
Slightly more experience/ confidence	Tell the person what your desired outcome is, and plan the steps together. Less frequent checkpoints than above.
More experienced, though needs some guidance and help	Tell the person what your desired outcome is and allow them to plan it, then establish when checkpoints are necessary.
Experienced, committed person	Explain the required outcome, timescales, and checkpoints (if any), and leave them to get on with it. But **don't** abdicate all responsibility for a task; you are the team leader, and are ultimately responsible for everything!

TOP TIP
The secret of good delegation (and supervision) is to put yourself into your team members' shoes. Imagine being a really capable professional who knows and enjoys what you're doing, but having a project

manager who's constantly peering over your shoulder and commenting on how you do your job! Conversely, think what it would be like for a new recruit, who's still very unsure of themselves and their role, to be managed by a 'hands-off' boss who leaves them to sink or swim. How would *you* react under those circumstances?

Step seven: Look at how it went

When a task is complete, give praise and review how things went. If an employee's responsibilities are increased as a result of a job well done, make sure as far as you can that he or she receives fair rewards for it. Make a note of what the person has achieved, so it's ready for appraisals or general feedback sessions: when it comes to making a case for your team member to have a salary increase, all of this will help you build a stronger argument in his or her favour.

On the other hand, if your team member has found the task delegated particularly challenging, or hasn't been able to deliver in the way you'd expected, discuss it with them, find out what went wrong, and aim to resolve problems in the future. Listen carefully to what they have to say and don't try to see the bigger picture: did he or she need more time, support, or an extra budget? What would help him or her to handle the task differently next time?

Common mistakes

✗ You think you 'haven't got time' to delegate

This is a very common reaction among people who are new to delegating, but try not to fall into this trap. It's particularly tempting to think like this if you're new to a job, as you may feel that others will think you can't cope if you don't do everything yourself. In fact, delegating less important or very time-consuming tasks to your new team is one of the best things you can do. It will free you up to concentrate on the big jobs to be done, and make your team feel that you trust them and want to involve them in what you're doing.

✗ You expect people to do things like you do

Managers often criticise the way things are done because it isn't the way they would have done it themselves. This is unreasonable and unfair. We all work in different ways, so try to concentrate on the *results* rather than the *methods used* to obtain them.

✗ You don't give people a chance

If you're giving someone something new to do, you must be patient. It'll take time for employees to develop new skills, but it's time that will pay off in the end. Have faith in the people around you.

✗ You delegate responsibility without authority

It's unfair to expect results from someone who has one hand tied behind his or her back. If you're going to delegate responsibilities, make sure that everyone else involved with this task knows this too. Make clear that the person you've delegated to is the contact person for all matters related to that task, and that you've given them the authority to get on with doing the job well.

STEPS TO SUCCESS

✔ Take every opportunity you can to delegate tasks to your team. You will all benefit from it.

✔ When you're delegating a task, take care to pick the right person for it, rather than hand out work randomly to the next person who passes your desk. If at all possible, tailor the tasks you delegate to people with the right skills, or those who have the potential to develop them.

✔ When you're discussing a task with the person who will be taking charge of it, give as much information as you can about what you are expecting, the deadline, and any other relevant information. Encourage your team member to ask as many questions as they need to in order to feel confident about it.

✔ Be ready to answer any extra queries as and when they come up. It's important to offer support while at the same time letting the other person get on with the job.

✔ Don't interfere if things are going well!

✔ When the task is over, review it with the team member, offering praise, feedback, and learning points as appropriate. Make a note of successes and let your own managers know.

✔ Bear in mind that you can delegate upwards too, if necessary.

Useful links

BusinessBalls:
www.businessballs.com/delegation.htm
'Delegating to Employees' by Carter McNamara:
**www.managementhelp.org/guiding/delegate/
delegate.htm**
MindTools.com, 'Successful Delegation':
www.mindtools.com/pages/article/newLDR_98.htm

Defusing tension within teams

Now for the final chapter in this team management crash course . . .

When any group of individuals comes together, there is the inevitable potential for disgruntlement, disagreement, and conflict. If such tensions are not tackled straight away, they can escalate out of control and disable a team.

Even if you follow the advice in the previous chapters to the letter, it doesn't guarantee a tension-free team. The unexpected can still happen, so it is as well to have a way of defusing tension in a team—not only to prevent its collapse, but also to increase its creativity. It's important to realise that defusing tension is not purely a preventive measure; tension can be a creative force, resulting in increased innovation and productivity.

Step one: Know the symptoms of team tension

It's simple: a team whose members are not enjoying a productive and enjoyable working relationship won't achieve its goals. Deadlines will be missed, factions will develop, and an unhealthy competitiveness could damage the team's work. The mood will be heavy and the team will lack enthusiasm and inventiveness. When asked, team members may even deny the problem—as acknowledgement suggests collusion. To help move things along, give your team direct feedback on your observations and feelings about the general ambience.

TOP TIP
A well-managed team should have terms of engagement which set out agreed methods of dealing with conflict. See chapter 5 for details.

Step two: Understand your team's conflict resolution preferences

There are some well-known approaches to resolving tensions which you might like to use to help you get the best from your team. One such approach recommends that you understand your team members' conflict resolution preferences.

Business writers Kenneth Thomas and Ralph Killman identified five main styles of dealing with conflict. They are:

- **Competitive.** This is a style used by those who know what they want and are prepared to use their power to ensure that they get it. It is a useful style when there is an urgent situation in which decision making must be rapid and the need for co-operation is paramount. This style generally has a short lifespan as people can end up feeling battered and bruised.
- **Collaborative.** Someone operating in this style will try to get everyone involved and make decisions by consensus. It is an assertive style which is both proactive and dynamic. People using this style are generally successful in bringing many viewpoints together and arriving at a mutually satisfying solution which has a long-term positive impact on the team.
- **Compromising.** This is the 'you give a little, I'll give a little' style of conflict management. It is useful in situations where there is a high risk of costly, damaging conflict.
- **Accommodating.** The accommodator tends to meet the needs of others at the expense of their own. They may be considered co-operative; but as they're unlikely to challenge those they consider more dominant than themselves, this passive style doesn't always lead to the best outcome.
- **Avoiding.** People adopting this style are generally conflict-averse and will avoid taking controversial decisions, either out of fear, or out of genuine concern for others' feelings. Whatever their reasons, the style is generally considered to be weak and does not contribute much to high-performing teams.

Although many of us have a preferred conflict style, being aware of preferences helps us to be flexible and adopt a different style when the situation demands it.

TOP TIP
Once you have deduced the protagonists'
conflict resolution preferences, you can
work out the best approach to take in
order to find a way forward.

Step three: Try the interest-based approach

Another approach to conflict management is the Interest-Based Relational (IBR) approach. This approach respects people's individuality while, at the same time, helping them avoid becoming too set in their ways.

Here are the rules of the IBR approach:

✔ **Good relationships are the priority.** Even if the pressure is high, treat your opponent calmly and respectfully. Try to remain constructive.

✔ **Focus on the problem, not on the personality.** Few people set out to be difficult. Generally, tensions arise because assumptions or values differ. Try to look at these objectively so that you can reveal the real reason behind the dispute.

✔️ **Listen attentively and understand the other's view.** Make an effort to be open to the other's opinion without judgement so that you can understand why they have taken the stand they have taken.

✔️ **Receive before you transmit.** Having heard the other's position, explain your own. Try not to be dismissive, scathing, or defensive.

✔️ **Establish some common ground.** If you can establish an area of agreement, you'll be able to identify the point at which your opinions diverge and the reasons for this.

✔️ **Explore the options.** You may have to relinquish your own preferred solution and find a third way to achieve your mutual objectives.

Step four: Meet to work through the problem

Call your team together and work through the stages below:

✔️ **Create the context.** As team leader, it's down to you to intervene when tensions are high—especially if the team are unable to resolve the tensions themselves. Outline the situation as you see it and give feedback on your perceptions. Be clear about the 'rules' and ensure that everyone listens attentively and respects each other's opinions. Encourage assertive communication, where people take responsibility for what they say.

✔ **Bring in all the relevant information.** Allow everyone's viewpoints to be made without judgement or intervention. Encourage team colleagues to air their assumptions, values, and motivations, and to offer constructive feedback. Focus on the impact of the conflict or tension and explore the consequences should it persist.

✔ **Restate the problem.** Once everyone is clear about the cause of the tension, restate the issue clearly so that you know where you're starting from. You need to get agreement on exactly what the problem is, as it may be perceived differently by different people. You should also state what you believe to be the desirable outcome and get agreement on this.

✔ **Explore possible solutions.** Get everyone to contribute their ideas and encourage a positive reception even if the idea seems ridiculous. Often the most unlikely ideas lead to the most creative resolution.

✔ **Agree a way forward.** Once everyone's position has been clarified, tensions often disappear by themselves. However, if you still need to work out a way forward, suggest a decision-making process and use this to find the best solution.

Step five: Encourage constructive feedback

Disagreement over goals and priorities generally ranks higher than personality clashes as the reason for team tension. Often this is due to unspoken assumptions about what these are or should be. Other people's views are sometimes diametrically opposed to our own; as this is unthinkable to us, we develop a 'blind spot' which prevents us from identifying, sharing, and discussing our differences.

One way of minimising tensions is to encourage a culture of instant constructive feedback. This prevents misunderstandings from building into something bigger than they warrant. By encouraging such a culture, you will help ideas to flow freely, avoid potential pitfalls, enhance efficiency, and address tensions before they become problems. A healthy team enjoys uninhibited, open communication that focuses not on personalities but on the means of reaching its goals.

TOP TIP
Don't get drawn into the conflict. If you judge that things are getting out of hand, take a step back and a deep breath, and try to look at the situation objectively.

Step six: Appreciate the value of successful resolutions

Silent co-operation is generally a conflict avoidance strategy, and is not a very productive approach to resolving tension. A diverse team, full of different interests, backgrounds, and opinions, is generally more dynamic. It may be harder to manage, but it will lead to greater success in the end.

The successful resolution of tensions will create a strong bond between team members, a more dynamic environment, and (hopefully!) a series of happy memories. Indeed, people often look back on their peak team experiences with nostalgia and wish that they could recreate and re-experience them.

Common mistakes

✗ You try to defuse tension where it could actually have a positive effect

In some situations, well-managed tension can cause a team to confront its disagreements and improve the quality of its decision making. This, in turn, leads to greater efficiency and effectiveness.

✗ You assume tensions are a team problem rather than a management problem

Although serious tensions might lead to an intervention from you in your role as team leader, you need to be aware that there may be very good reasons for the current state of affairs. For example, the team may not be clear on its goals; it may not have enough resources or people; role responsibilities may not be clear; or the schedule or budget may be too tight. Make sure you haven't missed anything obvious before you interpret tensions as a team problem.

✗ You don't communicate your assumptions and perceptions

Although a diverse team is rich in terms of its potential, behavioural tensions can be rooted in diversity. Power issues, assumptions, values, attitudes, and beliefs are all potential causes of tension within a team. The most common, however, is poor communication. This can be resolved by ensuring that everyone knows what part they are playing in the overall aspirations of the team.

✗ You think that all tension is bad

Every team goes through a period where tensions are high. It is generally referred to as the 'storming' phase of team development. Storming is a necessary stage on the way to becoming a high-performing team. Many talents, skills, and ideas are brought to the surface during this time and can be used to find unexpectedly inventive solutions and to achieve previously undreamed-of successes. To realise the potential of this stage, it should be well managed, not quelled because you want to return to the easier 'forming' stage when everyone is being co-operative and polite.

STEPS TO SUCCESS

✔ Appreciate that tension is inevitable.

✔ Don't allow tension to simmer unchecked.

✔ Remember that everyone reacts differently to conflict.

✔ Encourage your team to communicate in order to work through the tension.

✔ Appreciate that tension, well managed, can result in a more positive team approach.

Useful links

MindTools.com: 'Conflict resolution':
www.mindtools.com/pages/article/newLDR_81.htm
Innovative Team Building: 'Resolving conflict in work teams':
www.innovativeteambuilding.co.uk/pages/articles/conflicts.htm
Thomas Killman Conflict Mode Instrument (click on 'Psychometric Tools' then 'Personality'):
www.opp.eu.com/index.aspx

Where to find more help

**The Inspirational Leader:
How to Motivate, Encourage and
Achieve Success**
John Adair
Kogan Page, 2005
208pp ISBN: 0749444568
This book explores the nature and practice of leadership
and reinforces the author's argument that leaders are not
born but made. It takes the form of conversations between
a young chief executive and the author. Each aspect of
leadership is studied and discussed so that the key skills
are revealed for anyone to adopt and use.

**Management Teams:
Why They Succeed or Fail:
2nd edition**
R. Meredith Belbin
Butterworth-Heinemann, 2003
224pp ISBN: 0750659106
R. Meredith Belbin is an international expert on teams
and the way they work. In this influential book he analyses
and discusses many different kinds of teams and team
behaviours. There are also a range of case studies of
Belbin's theories in action and a self-assessment so that
readers can match their own personalities to particular
team roles. This is essential reading for any manager who
wants to achieve real results by getting the best from his
or her team members.

The Wisdom of Teams
Jon Katzenbach
McGraw-Hill, 2005
336pp ISBN: 0077111680

This book is the result of research into why teams are important, what distinguishes effective from ineffective teams, and how organisations can use strong-performing teams to become strong-performing companies. Using research into 47 organisations, Katzenbach and Smith explain their views as to what makes teams work, and how this can be transferred to the reader's own workplace.